Wild Weather

Thunderstorms

by Julie Murray

Dash!
LEVELED READERS

3

Dash!
LEVELED READERS

Level 1 – Beginning
Short and simple sentences with familiar words or patterns for children who are beginning to understand how letters and sounds go together.

Level 2 – Emerging
Longer words and sentences with more complex language patterns for readers who are practicing common words and letter sounds.

Level 3 – Transitional
More developed language and vocabulary for readers who are becoming more independent.

abdopublishing.com

Published by Abdo Zoom, a division of ABDO, P.O. Box 398166, Minneapolis, Minnesota 55439.
Copyright © 2018 by Abdo Consulting Group, Inc. International copyrights reserved in all countries.
No part of this book may be reproduced in any form without written permission from the publisher.

Printed in the United States of America, North Mankato, Minnesota.
092017
012018

Photo Credits: iStock, Shutterstock
Production Contributors: Kenny Abdo, Jennie Forsberg, Grace Hansen, John Hansen
Design Contributors: Dorothy Toth

Publisher's Cataloging in Publication Data
Names: Murray, Julie, author.
Title: Thunderstorms / by Julie Murray.
Description: Minneapolis, Minnesota: Abdo Zoom, 2018. | Series: Wild weather |
    Includes online resource and index.
Identifiers: LCCN 2017939261 | ISBN 9781532120893 (lib.bdg.) | ISBN 9781532122019 (ebook) |
    ISBN 9781532122576 (Read-to-Me ebook)
Subjects: LCSH: Thunderstorms--Juvenile literature. | Weather--Juvenile literature. | Environment—
    Juvenile literature.
Classification: DDC 551.55--dc23
LC record available at https://lccn.loc.gov/2017939261

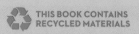

Table of Contents

Thunderstorms 4

How They Form 10

Stay Safe 18

More Facts 22

Glossary 23

Index 24

Online Resources 24

Thunderstorms

A flash of light goes across the sky. A loud BOOM follows it. What is happening? A thunderstorm! There are about 2,000 thunderstorms occurring around the world at any given moment.

Thunderstorms are storms with rain, lightning, and thunder.

They happen most often during
the spring and summer months.
This is because thunderstorms
need warm, humid air to form.

Most thunderstorms are not **severe**. They usually only last about 30 minutes. Severe thunderstorms include hail and wind. Sometimes, they even produce tornadoes.

If it keeps growing, it can become a tropical storm. Some of these storms grow into hurricanes, while others die out.

How They Form

Thunderstorms happen when warm, humid air rises above cold air. This forms cumulonimbus clouds. These clouds are tall with flat tops. Some can be 10 miles (16 km) high!

A lot of energy builds up in these clouds. This energy is electricity and it turns into lightning. The lightning heats the air around it and causes the air to expand. This produces the loud noise of thunder.

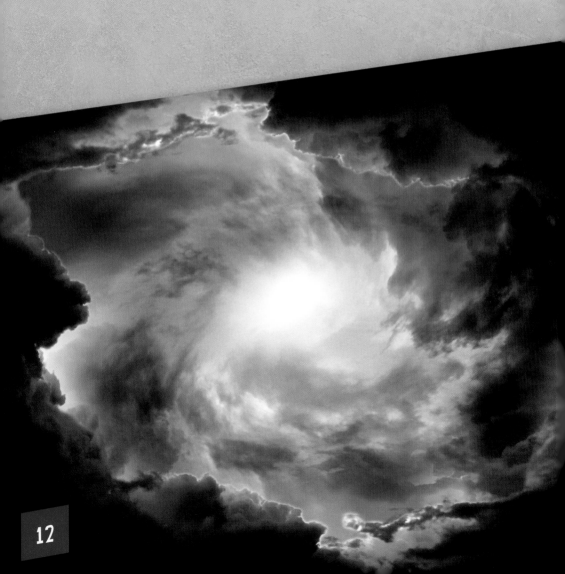

Lightning and thunder happen at the same time. Light moves faster than sound, so we see lightning first.

How far away is the lightning?
Sound travels about one mile
(1.6 km) in five seconds.

Count the seconds between the lighting and thunder. Then divide it by five. If you count up to ten, the lightning is two miles (3.2 km) away (10/5=2).

Stay Safe

Meteorologists use tools such as satellites, radars, and **weather balloons** to track storms. They can warn people that a thunderstorm is in their area.

It is important to get inside a building or a car during a thunderstorm. The lightning can be deadly! If you can't get inside, be sure to stay away from water, metal, and tall objects.

- About 100 lightning bolts hit the earth each second.

- Lightning is five times hotter than the surface of the sun.

- There are about 16 million thunderstorms in the world each year.

Glossary

meteorologist – a weather forecaster.

severe – very strong or intense.

weather balloon – a balloon used to carry instruments into the sky to gather meteorological data in the atmosphere.

Index

air 7, 12

cloud 10

duration 8

formation 7, 10

hail 8

light 14

lightning 6, 12, 14, 16, 17, 21

meteorologist 19

rain 6

safety 19, 21

season 7

sound 14, 16

thunder 6, 12, 14, 17

wind 8

Online Resources

Booklinks
NONFICTION NETWORK
FREE! ONLINE NONFICTION RESOURCES

To learn more about thunderstorms, please visit **abdobooklinks.com**. These links are routinely monitored and updated to provide the most current information available.